KaSandra L. Turner

Eden

Reclaiming your divinity
through poetry and self-expression

Written by KaSandra Turner

Eden Copyright © by KaSandra Turner. All rights reserved. This book or any portion thereof may not be reproduced in any electronic, written, or photocopying. Its contents may not be recorded, stored, or copied for professional, personal, public or private use in any manner whatsoever. No part of this book or its contents is meant to encourage self-harm or the harm of others. Definitions used are from the artist's perspective based on their personal experiences and artistic expression. These definitions should not be taken literally. The contents of this book may be briefly quoted for book reviews.
ISBN: 978-0-578-90414-6

Author, cover art and illustrations: KaSandra Turner
Cover and illustration editor: Shareny Plaza

Websites and social media:
MAGICK OF EDEN Apothecary
Herbs, Ritual Oils and more at magickofeden.com
Instagram: @magickofeden

To the waters that nourish me
To the suns that kiss my petals
To those who help me grow

May you be loved
with Divine love. Always!

−Kassy ♡

The Garden:

Thorns
2

Withered
50

Tulips
86

Jasmines
114

Lotus
150

A Note from Eden
196

Tribe,

Thank you for being open and vulnerable with me on this journey. Your desire to listen and connect with me moves my soul around mountains. I hope that through these words you know that your pain is noticed. I hope the aura of togetherness fills your heart as you realize that you are never alone. The magnitude of my gratitude for dwelling in this moment with you is beyond what words can express. My intent is that you discover the peace that is already within you. I intend to share pieces of my past with you so that we can marvel at how far we've come in our lives. Thank you, Divine for your inspiration. You are the reason for this book. Our experiences have led us to this precious moment.

Asé

Thorns

Thorns

Pain | suf-fer-ing |

feeling:

- a piercing state of agony and discomfort

KaSandra Turner

Oppression Maybe?

On the day where the sun
slapped me awake
I sat up feeling empty
Like stomachache empty
nauseous with the fate
of meeting a reflection's gaze
of unsatisfactory skin
painted with the beatings of them
I must have been ten
when I shrugged to the room
designed to lay away your waste
and wash away your sins
Only my sins swam secretly
from my crown to my toes
who left stains for prints
on that screaming cold floor
I opened the door
and that wind shoved me in
A coward I was
to soap my hands and hide
from that reflection
who exposes the fears
in my dilated pupils
Things just seemed
much better looking down
at the dirt escaping
from my fingertips and prints
as it rushes through the pipes

Thorns

leading to a land of vast waste
I envy that dirt
It belongs somewhere
It has its place
and I belong nowhere
except between four walls dancing
with my knowing that I deserve
the opposite of gold's value and worth.

It's such a perilous pity that at the innocent age of four I knew what rejection felt like. I was a joke to adults because of my skin and smiles. I was trained to mask my pain at the precious age of six. How was I supposed to grow normal in a world that told me I was unworthy before I hit puberty?

Fix Me

They won't hold on to me
Maybe I'm just too fragile
They used me as their therapy
because the love I gave was free

They won't hold on to me now
Their love shatters easily
Since the love I gave was free,
I told them to fix me.

KaSandra Turner

Water Me

Why do you make me feel so small?
Why do you pluck away my leaves?
Why do you scatter all my seeds
and refuse to water me?

You've got the nerve tell them all
that your heart is big and tall
I refuse to agree,
just until you water me.

Self-Talk

Why do you gift me with neglect?
Why do you despise me?
Why do you constantly reflect
on insecurities that paralyze me?

All I do is for you
I reassure you that you matter
All that we've been through
still my words you scatter

It's bad enough they hate us
as if our existence is wrong
Maybe you are right
we really don't belong.

BreakMetoFixYou

*Our eyes are melted glass
in the scorching claws
of etchers
sculpting marbles
that crack in their reflections
Their bladed nails reach short
of their own backs
so they crack grins and sins
to those within reach
to mend and pretend
they're fixed when we break
They hide behind veils
and exhale
ghosts of grief
to float on the boats
of our dancing heartbeats
They break us beautifully
to beat their own
heartfelt drums.*

Thorns

I spent most of my early life laughing through my haunted cries. I wasted my energy diving into others striving to mold myself to their liking. My mind and body became enemies in the process. My flesh was abstract and unworthy of gazing each time I stared in the mirror.

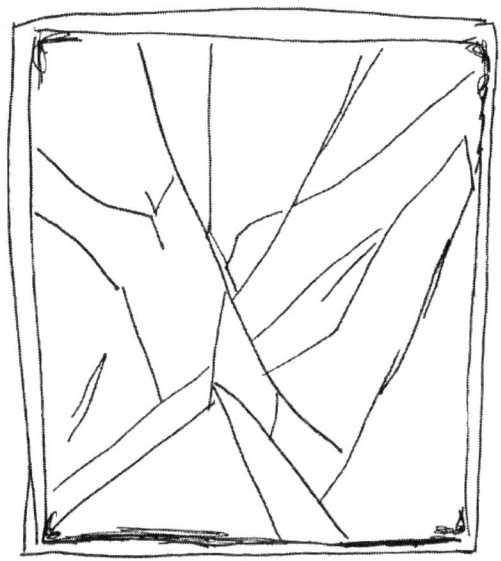

Stranger to a Soul

How easy it is to be a stranger
to the world rejecting
the best of insecurities
How easy it is to be a stranger
to the reflection housing
the best of complexities

Even the deer who drinks
at the toes of the riverbed
knows the soul that shines
along those sparkling ripples
How divine it must be
to have such a pair of eyes.

Nightmare of a Dream

I avoid my reflection in the river
as waterfalls rage down my cheeks
The poems of my tongue are bitter
when it's my eyes I meet
Disgust fills the pits of their guts
when their eyes lay upon my skin
The erosion of my sin is a must
How dare I find the peace within?

The thorns of my roses slice deep
in the flesh of those who pluck
My roots wither and weep
melting memories into muck
Sprouting through cracks of concrete
seems to be what's left for me
in this mysterious land of thought
A nightmare of a dream.

Telling yourself you reek of disappointment because you effortlessly failed to be who they are and who they failed to be.

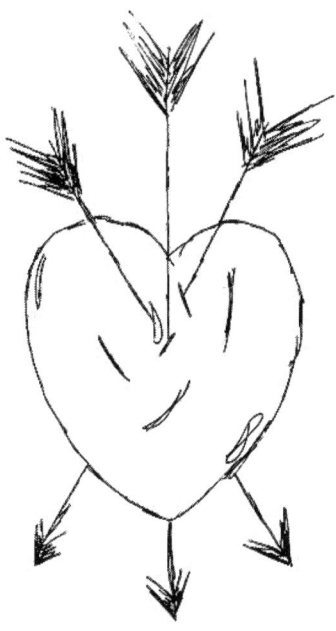

Blindfold

Snap my twig of a heart
in two and tarnish her
to dusted crumbles
Blade my branches in pleasure
as your sins
invade my existence
and deplete my being
Claw my confidence
with the ache
of your withered wishes
to be wanted and held
to breasts
that expel spells that tell
nothing
of your afflicted fingers
that focus on frictions
of your turbulent memories of ten
Win me over
with your bleeding need to be
the one who kills me most when
your chastity is devoured alive
How I wish we'd trade eyes.

KaSandra Turner

Triggered to Fear

My shoulders are anchored
with the weight of your oppressions
that dismantle my terrarium
of scavenged pieces
Parts of me drift
into the naked night
of fallen leaves as I breathe
in crisp clouds
in tingling crowds of fear
I dearly hold
the trust that dreams
cloaked in cellophane sheets
is all that is left of me
which you take for you
You beat me til' my cheeks stain blue
because the reality of my gift,
my power
could turn the globe
into a beating heart.

Thorns

She stopped breathing for herself
when she discovered that the world's needs
weighed heavy against hers on a scale. Her
own well-being became a mystery when
she started living through the eyes of
others.

KaSandra Turner

Hoping

Pleasing them is like
hoping for Sequoia trees
planting dying seeds

Thorns

Internal

I have yet to remember the day
I started to hate the hairs
prickling on my back and legs
I guess I may have started
when I was pulled into the world's sizzling chains
deeper than the oceans gaze
on a full moon in July
I cried and coveted
to be wrapped in wings
that carried my curses
away from the sweet melody
of my own flame that stings and pierces
the trust I have in my might
I sacrificed my strength
the day I heard the news
of the town that would rather outcast me
Submission to their ideals
replaced my power
because I found that my weakness
was grander than confrontation
Confusion often kissed the soles
of my breathing feet when I'd meet
their eyes, you see I was trained
to submit to that power higher than me
through yelling and screaming
and what felt like beatings
My feelings were never valid
only dismissed

by the ruler of my throne at home
Or maybe she understood sometimes
on the days I cried

Each day the clouds rested on the treetops
I scorned through my window
and leveled a torch within the caves
of my howling chest because what was best
was that I expressed my hurts in silence
Silence was more convenient for them,
for her because they all dreamed
of the days they could dance away their sins
on musty red carpets covered in cigarettes
if it meant releasing their own faults and regrets
There were days I wished to climb to the rooftop
of my project apartments and declare my hatred
for the world
for her, him and me
scream and jump to meet the end of me!
There were days I wished they'd find me hanging
scarred and naked from a tree
with a note that reads,
I just want to be loved and kissed
and seen as beauty like the other girls
and be loved with a love
that doesn't sting or bruise
physically or emotionally
I just want to be seen
As worthy of life
As love
As human

Thorns

I remain muzzled by my own might
despite my daring, daunting desire
to be treated with reverence
and seen in an angels light
Yet, I find my feet pacing right
into the nightmares of those
with whipped backs and eager hands
dying to strangle
the little life left in begging beings
as a means to cope with their untamed
shadows in wolves skin
How can I discover my truth
when all I see is black when I stare within?
How do I trust the light outside of me
when it just burns and pierces my dreams?
How do I cope and free my soul
when every corner carries curses
that creep and seep through every layer
of my cracked concrete of a heart?

I look at her sometimes
with a belly full of spiders
dying to be consoled
without the reminder of her afflictions
and how she showed strength
at a child's age
I want so gravely to giggle with others
without the vexing that follows
Yet, this strife that seals
its head and kneels
at the knees of my
conquered combats reveal

KaSandra Turner

that my screams
are better off left
internal.

Thorns

They look at me and laugh
I see them and smile
Maybe what they sense is weakness
A brittle twig for a hammer.

Dark Skin

There's a sort of funny giggling
from pretty gals pacing in midnight
during streetlight hours
Their peach bodies devour the hour
Dark leather feathers
swallow silent skins
that die in daylight
They'd rather howl at night
below a heightened voluminous moon
wearing black and blue
Blue is my baffled heart
when she sees seas of curly haired girls
with good hair and skin of white silk
I sit discouraged when the mirror
reflects towards me
I bleed when I hear them
down the street
mocking the worst parts of me
I often dream
of wearing matching shirts and sheets
at parties to party
and talk about nails, cats and hats
Instead I'm seen as thrown away toys
to pretty little flowers
lighter than the sun's gold.

Thorns

There are those who prey on the innocent because they are guilty of possessing sick and dominating sexual desires.
Set them on fire.

KaSandra Turner

Her Pain is Mine

I can only imagine having the precious skin
meant to be deflowered by my King of Cups
sliced by the predator sleeping in my grandma's bed
as a princess with bows and barrettes
I know that surely,
precisely with a penny's luck
that the horrors of those memories
would evade my sleep ruthlessly
I'd wear them like beasts wearing skins of beasts
Only I wouldn't share the shame underneath
that dead skin with the ones who came from me
by striking my hammer from Odin on a bad day
I swear I just want her to be okay
I want so badly to say,
Mommy I see you
It's going to get better
Like when the rabbits come out and eat carrots
and crunch on candy from fairies and mermaids
Like on the movies when the families
have dinners together
while singing, laughing and playing
We just have to give it time
Only now her pain is mine.

He Forgot to Pay

He stripped her of her toys and dresses
He cheated her of flesh
He left a million messes
when she was just a princess

He now sleeps beneath the grass
Free of doubts and worry
Before this came to pass
he never said, *I'm sorry*

She chose to welcome other men
despite her beasts of scars
When she forgot to go within
her blood burned black and tarred.

KaSandra Turner

Like earthy brown
eyes and copper skin,
some things
are passed down
waiting to shine
and rest upon
your spine.

He stared into my innocent soul and decided that it was my time to know the process of creating life. He consoled me and asked, *do you know what sex is?*

I nervously swayed my head from shoulder to shoulder. He gently tapped the jeans between his legs and replied soothingly, *it's when you stick this... into this,* while gently tapping me below my pants line with the tip of his index finger. The same finger he used between his own legs.

He was so proud. I hadn't yet discovered my period...

Innocence

He watched her innocence
He kept her concealed
from other youth on those days
to be comforted by her laughs
and wits for her age
He bathed her on those nights
like the stars bathe the sky
Taught her of her womanhood
before the blood could escape her womb,
before her breasts became full.

A fool she was when she was young
to play with her dolls
to create her world of joy
He had another plan that day
During snack time,
she was blinded with that cotton cloth
to enjoy that chocolate popsicle
He smiled in delight
through her naivety

When she finally discovered
her womanhood
that moment she suppressed, resurfaced
She knew with no proof
the things he had done
She grew broken as a woman.

Thorns

I had to peer into my brother's eyes and see his father, the man that took half of my purity. I saw the eyes, nose and lips of this monster formed together annoyingly perfect upon his face. As if staring into this entity wasn't enough, I was told to conceal my molestation. I was told to lie when asked all for another's comfort and convenience. I was drunk with fear. Of course I complied.

Does it Count?

I keep quiet and silenced
when another woman describes
how her insides screamed
because it felt like someone
jacked her pearls
and scrapped them against
concrete repeatedly
He forced her to do things
involuntarily

He didn't gut my insides
physically at least
So, does it make a difference
if it's not penetration?
Is it still molestation?
A violation?

Thorns

We are prized with oppression from our neighbors as if whips from the ones we love most isn't enough. We are stabbed and slaughtered with the fears projected onto us by fragile beings with blades for nails. We stay gentle and rooted in the fear of being blamed and condemned by the world if we released our rapture.

Hell is at home. The world is hell. These are both places that we dwell. How do we welcome peace and free ourselves?

-I need answers

Their Pain Means More

We seek survival by comparing
our distress to other lives
We seek comfort by staring
through the twine of other vines
We fear that our fears are diminished
if they lack the same feathers as others
We live through the lack of
remembrance of our own history,
uncovered.

Thorns

The hate we've learned
is held dear
as fears passed down
to other seeds.

KaSandra Turner

We have been born to absorb
our parents' oppressions
We are gifted shields
that house them
from their afflictions.

We bleed when our mothers
and fathers are wounded
They are unhealed children,
traumatized, alone and afraid.

Love Me Gently

How hurt you are my love
to cry storms on your sheets
drifting off into your dreams
of agony
You try to love the life you created
instead you strike me
sometimes when you're angry

My heart aches too
So does my skin sometimes
when you're livid
I'm so sorry that you're hurting
I know that you're trying,
but you're hurting me
I know they wounded you
they will pay
But, please love me gently today
You don't see the pain you cause
How can you
when you're memories marinate
in your scars?

I am your outlet
and maybe that's okay
I trust that you'll love me
gently one day

KaSandra Turner

The times you bruised me and yelled you called it love.
The times you cursed me out you called it discipline.

You failed to apologize for this toxicity, and I grew to confuse anger with love.

Thorns

What Love Made You Do

You say you scream to keep from hurting us
as if screaming doesn't sting
You say that being hard is a must
as if being gentle is the wrong thing
I admit there were moments you tried
the nights you sent me to my room
Because of your pain I was blind
There was no way you could bloom.
To you being hard was a must
because you refused for us to be you
Instead you caused distrust
given everything we've been through
You say we'll forever be your babies
even when your heart stops beating
There is no doubt, no maybe
that this cycle kept repeating.

The bruises, the scrapes and screams
tell me, were they worth it?
Because according to my self-esteem
it seems I need better judgement
The worst part about it all
is that we matured with no closure
No therapist to call
when we couldn't hold our composure.

My mind still bleeds these seeds
even though I'm older now
And I'm starting to believe

KaSandra Turner

that this life is but a vow
I despise them for your wounds
that you effortlessly revealed
Through your lonesome you presumed,
that you need to be healed

I will forever love you,
me and my brothers
We will always have a place for you
After all
your name is Mother.

I'm Afraid of You

I am your child
The flesh formed from within your womb
Instead I feel like a punching bag
absorbing the electricity
of your wounding words and whips
You taught me to fear your rumbling,
your rapture
What you failed to realize
was that I may never come to trust you
I would be writing in a diary
that everyone has a key to
I would see you as the soul
out to get me when you were scared
I would never trust you to be my mother
in the ways I need you most.

KaSandra Turner

They took us away that night.
They separated me and my brothers
like split peas.
My eyes pored
as I slept in a house
full of strangers
like me.

Thorns

I haven't many memories with you, dad. So, I searched for you in the boys I met. They gave me attention and forced me into a begging peasant pleading for their approval. I was a slave to their insecurities while searching and waiting for you.

I needed you there to protect me. To show me the ways of sneaky little boys and how to trick them if they tormented me. I thought you'd be there to sweep me off my feet and stay.

I'm still waiting for the day where you teach me to play chess. King's gambit, I guess.

KaSandra Turner

I gaze into your eyes
through my reflection
We look just alike
Thick, dark hair
chocolate skin
branches broken.

Thorns

It was that night where Lilith lit the heavens and dewy sprouts whispered secrets to my memories.
Leftover food at Grandma's house lingered through my aunt's room where I slept on vacation.
My stepmother's cries waved within the walls.
I finally understand why she was so stressed those mornings she made us eggs.

KaSandra Turner

I often wondered why
you weren't around all those years
I suppose you were busy
suppressing your tears
Real men don't cry,
you said that day
I guess this was the reason
you stayed away

    -Daddy's Logic

Thorns

The least protected
loves and protects the most
despite the utmost
paralyzing sting,
gifted to the blades of our
backs.

How sweet it is
that the ones we birth
present us with endearing oppressions
their enemies engraved in their hearts
Yet, we're expected to birth this world
and nurture broken wings

When will we be loved as though we matter?
Don't we matter?
How beautifully erroneous
these thoughts choose to be.

Loyalty

Don't only choose to protect the ones
your desires crave
Don't only choose to uplift women
with wide hips
your fingertips can sing to
Don't let your protection end
where our dark skin begins.
We are your mothers,
your daughters,
your sisters,
grandmothers and ancestors
who cloak you in love and protection!
We sacrifice our sanity
ensuring your safety
and pave a path that leads you
to your throne.
Despite your learned hatred for us
we genuinely,
passionately,
and unapologetically
choose to love you.

Withered

Depression | numb - ness |
state of being:

- existing in a realm of darkness that leads to dejection
- your body's way of pleading for recovery

Goodbye

Give me a reason to clench a hand
or please help me to let go
I'd rather know
what was on the other side

I'd rather dance in the black,
the unknown
For at least I'll be known
as goodbye.

Opposing Hearts

I war with you to keep my sane buried
beneath the soil,
yet you shovel me with your apathy
I fight to keep my branches strong,
yet you snap them with
your loathe for me
I struggle miserably
to keep the peace
due to my love
for the fruit of different trees
They all exist beautifully
They bathe under the same sun
and drink of the same skies
despite their uniqueness

I perceive you as a part of me
because this gift called duality
is what makes our thoughts dance
in symphony
How unfortunate that you see
with a heart separate from me.

Withered

To be so far gone
that you can barely feel
your breath and body
To be seduced by claws so gripping
that your screams bounce off
the craters of the moon
Only the screaming
dwells inside your mind
To be choked with the rusted blades
of your childhood fears
appears
to be the only reasons worth living.

Space Time

Enslaved in a space time domain
I remain detached from the core
that radiates the flame
whose mission calls to lead me
from this sunken place
This barely perceivable light
with a radiance that exerts its might
fails effortlessly to raise me
from my demise

Being drowned in poisonous potions
of plastic rivers that run and stream
from the mouths and deeds of deceiving,
diluted dreams
is but a positive reinforcement
for my dancing in crystalline patterns
of my oppressors' distortions
Fractals of dense agony
evade my essence and anchor my will
to the sea floor of sins
that nurture and cocoon me in thrill
How did I become entangled
in the web of false ideologies
created by false lords who rape and kill
without apologies?
Is this life of my own choosing
to ensure my adaptability and evolution?
Is this even life,

Withered

or is it merely a perpetual hell
as punishment for a karmic cycle?

As if the war amongst minds wouldn't suffice
I was enslaved in the heisting
of my purity
There is no up, down, left
or anything relative
Just the darkness whose pulse rings
with a sullen beat
That fire whose mission remains unfulfilled
still
kisses the tongue of defeat

Dread seduces my senses
in sadistic pleasure
and not one other single strand of thought
seems to empathize
or is even aware of this pain
This acid rain
that melts my skin down to bone
remains almost invisible
like that barely perceivable light
with a radiance that exerts its might

I'll remain enslaved in this sunken place
this space time domain
waiting for infinity to repeat itself
proudly again.

KaSandra Turner

My soul is hooked with bladed chains
of laughing grief spiraling down
an avenue of shattered screams.

Withered

Unknown Haiku

Perpetual states
Of obscurity must be
Fine for me for sure

The Things I Never Told Them

I often ache for an experience where I wonder in a dimension alone away from all the chaos and demands of other humans. I sometimes numbly sit hunch backed on man-made stone imagining a scenery of ponds, daisies and creatures who judge based off the laws of nature. I often vision a heaven with a nebula forming the sky and horizon meeting a glistening sea's touch. It's there I'll be embraced.

There are days where I get so sick to my stomach of this energy, I become paralyzed and numb. I can't tell if I'm breathing, awake or sleeping. Food is pointless. The only thing weighing me to the planet is the pool of dense thoughts that blanket my aura.

Our planet is half the size of a grain of sand in this universe and somehow, I feel I take up too much space. I feel that my existence is an inconvenience and that I'm a disgrace. A sham. A shame to be around let alone to look at. Looking down won't save me from the sharp truth that I'm too weird and ugly to be around. This is precisely why I don't fit in and can't stand crowds. I just feel so unworthy and the only one who would welcome me with a yearning vengeance is oblivion. She'll swallow me whole and force me to let go. Shell claw and tear me open and consume me from the inside out.

I often get overlooked in conversations as if my presence triggers their annoyance. Just the fact that I'm breathing bothers people and I genuinely believe that my mother made a mistake in keeping me. That she should have aborted the mission. What is it about me that makes people despise and reject me?

Withered

I stare into the presence of other humans and I see beauty in their skin and eyes. I see the potential they have to be Gods yet all they see in me is something to mock and make fun of for being obscure.

I loathe this place and this society molded from plastic. How ironic that I too, wish to be made from the same cellophane.

KaSandra Turner

Right and left cease to exist
in this plain of infinite movement
All that is dear to me
are waves of destitution
In conclusion,
ambient songs of confusion
will suffice in this illusion.

Sleepwalking

I sometimes lie on concrete springs
while my black blankets hard and heavy
cascade their way over my chest and knees
The ceiling stares into my sorrowed brows
as I inhale the sting
of the air's silent songs and rings
When the sun finds his way through my curtains
I rise with survival gripping my prints
pulling me into another fractal state
of bewildered streams
I often find myself barely breathing
while walking on cotton clouds
that float above flaming rivers
of screeching souls
desperate for consolation
For their internal desolation
is all that they've known
All that we've known

We are guided by eyes
programmed by popes and people
who encourage us to perceive false stimuli as real
We just want to be led
because pacing our own path
is obscure and foreign
We rise to walk in dreams
oblivious to the dismantling
and destruction exposed in symbols

on our billboards and TV screens
We willingly submit
to a bloodthirsty kingdom of false gods
that we naively sacrifice our power to
in exchange for a life
that would wither in a matter of minutes
if they lifted even a pinky nail
We slowly drag the soles of our shoes
with our heads held straight
and eyes forced open
with the sizzling burn of survival
clawing through our spines
Our shoulders are stuck and compressed
like organs rearranged from too little corsets

When will we realize that as an elevated species,
a billion hearts beating simultaneously
that we are mighty and brilliant
If only we would wake from their nightmares
acknowledge our dreams
and play our own beats
together forming an orchestra,
a symphony
we'd dismantle them and weaken their knees

I yearn for a beauty that captivates
and makes people listen willingly
If I had a stage set
and a platform that stretches
across the pacific
I would tell my truth,

Withered

my revelations and prophecies of us
all loving and showing empathy
and compassion
like the purple that prances
on an orchid's petals with passion
I would reveal the divine's love and wisdom
in that beetle on a windowsill
like the leaf that brushes against your wrist
who reveals
a set of complexities that are mirrored
in our bloodstreams

Despite my burn for a cosmic family
that dwells together
in a garden of life everlastings
singing songs and reaching nirvana,
I'll remain amongst sentient beings
robbed of their consciousness
I'll remain here and sympathize
alongside my sisters and brethren
unkempt in dazzling eyes

KaSandra Turner

I ache for solitude
in the dead hours of midnight
to be numbed by cold
thoughts.

This diseased state of mind is
ever so kind to comfort me
Please, leave me alone tonight.

Withered

Cliffhanging

When I meet their souls I sense potential,
but their masks are glittered
with rejection for me
Their silent thoughts screech through my skin
even though their lips stand quietly
I extend my palms
to remind them of my knowing
of this lonesome life
Perhaps I fail to see
that these extensions of me
live dreams that beam with glee
How fulfilled they are without memories of me

My heart walks tall and extends its warmth
to those close and afar
But what sense does this make
to extend my love to those
who'll live better days without me anyway?
So, here I lay
belly caressing the knobby ground
at the tip of this cliff
with tears seeping through my pores
Here I lay with oceans flowing
to my fingertips
as hope is slipping, drifting
and falling away from me.

Angels and Demons

I have dwelt in the hells of a demon's gaze
I have walked with angels in an infinite maze
Those demons wore the truth atop their blades

These dangerous demons sang truths with fiddles
Those angels left pebbles prized with riddles
I remained sunken, drained and belittled

Those hell hounds and ferocious beings of light
Were twins and triplets possessed with missions
They ripped my soul and destroyed my sight

Some demons project their power and will
Some angels protect their master's will
Still, I remain a bird without flight

Look at Me!

Hey, look at me!
Can you tell by the way I stretch my lips
wide like the horizon
that I'm hiding the burn of a drooping gaze?
Can you feel beyond
the contagious crying laughter
escaping from my dying womb
who's pregnant with dense shadows
tormenting and tearing my insides
ferociously?

Hey, look at me!
Can you tell by the cackling of my cheeks
who move like chains dancing on concrete
that I'm burdened with concealing
the devil that drapes down my spine
to protect you from my whimpering whines?
Can you hear beyond the music
of comedy squeezing through my teeth?
Do you hear the pleading?
Can you see the bleeding?

I know you'll be surprised,
shook and pierced
if you found me lifeless
with red tears stained on my chin
I know you'll blame yourself
for not peering through my facade

KaSandra Turner

You wouldn't be blamed

I will pray to someone's God
through the snot, tears and sobs
that you'll never find me that way
But, please I beg of you
look at me.

Withered

To tell the stories
of your wounds and trauma
in the light of this world
may cost you a life or two
And if not, it may cost you
a relationship or two,
or three, or four.

How do we proceed
when this fate awaits?
How do we go on
when we are gifted
with so many ways to die?

I suppose that dwelling
in the light of the shadows
is also a good way to go
At least they know
the truth.

KaSandra Turner

I'd rather tie a slipknot
with no fingers
than vocalize my afflictions
I get triggered at the reality
that this life of mine
You gifted me
must be mended by no one I
I beg for help
And yet, death seems to be
more reassuring than any
promise
We all make mistakes, but this?
I'd rather not be awake

-Random thoughts throughout the day

Withered

The grass gives the rain a chance
to race from the clouds
Sunflowers wait willingly
to meet the sun's gaze in the east
Cliffs keep calm and still
waiting for the sea
to slap against their structures at will
These are perfect symphonies,
all in which I may never understand.

KaSandra Turner

There are days
where I yearn to walk away
from it all
While the wind carries my footprints
to the stars
While the moon raises the tides
of my tears
While the night reveals
my fears.
Instead I stay
glued to this seat of sadness
It is here I'll stay
I promise I'll make it

-I just need time

Withered

I remain quiet after you speak.
My silence rings louder than your laugh.
When you close your eyes for a kiss, I stare.
I swear I care, just leave me.

KaSandra Turner

I was a feast to feed your own shortcomings
I was the rag to wipe the filth from your shoes
I was the flash to light a way to you
Now look at me,
distressed just like you.

Giving Up

Lay me at that resting place
where nothing and everything exists
Where every note played
sings together, a cosmic song
Lay me at that resting place
free of racing thoughts
Free of whimpering judgements
of those who fail to be

I have no more of my mind to give
I have no more of my life to live
Take me to that resting place
to lay at the feet of freedom.

KaSandra Turner

I sometimes sit and stare at the walls
with a cringing stomach
closed nostrils
and burning eyes
wondering why
it's not yet my time...

Withered

Shapeshifter

Depression has shown
Itself as a shapeshifter
I have been deceived

KaSandra Turner

*My conscience scolds me when I fail to comfort
you. Your screams deepen the caves of my heart.
My attempts to mother you ache in vain.
Please my baby, show me how to love you.*

Postpartum

They sliced me open
due to their hunger for coins
I took you home
painting my traumas
like clowns at a carnival
dancing for a band of toddlers
I limp and bend on my way to you
despite that truth
that I have no strength or will of my own
to refresh my bandages
carelessly consuming the blood
trickling down my crying womb
I can barely latch you
to the source of which your nourishment flows
and I know
it's not your fault
You are my blessing
and for this very reason
I can see I'm not a blessing to you

The throbbing of my breast and scars
are myths because I am wonder woman
At least that's what the world
will beat me into
if I fail to meet their unrealistic standards
if I express my aching neck and tiredness
I just wish you had someone more worthy
of your love and dedication

KaSandra Turner

You've only been here two weeks
and I'm failing as your mother.
I can't do this
Someone please,
help me...

You Deserve More

I wonder if my care is enough
You play with your toys
we converse in laughter
Still I feel the need to do more
When you're asleep I stare, smiling
until my heart storms
with inadequacy.

You deserve so much better
than what I can offer
You deserve so much better than me
I'm so sorry
that I cannot be
all that you need.

When our ancestors paced the planet, our tribes were in sync. Women would be so in tune and trusting of each other that they would care for another's baby. If one couldn't breastfeed then another would nourish the child and teach their sisters, their daughters and granddaughters the ways of motherhood.

Now we kill each other behind a screen with little racing Venom F5's for thumbs. We bypass each other's struggles because we should already know better. Apparently, we were born with a mother's manual.

Motherhood was such a gift to our foremothers. A part of some their legacies. Now it just makes you a target. The art has somehow become a nightmare.

Withered

After all the whips and drowning in the blood of my own tears, fears and self-inflicted oppressions something has to change. This addiction to the torture and emotional beatings needs to be broken. I can no longer follow this path of destruction. I'm done being consumed.

KaSandra Turner

Depression is the perception that consumes my essence. It is my choice to leave or to stay in this hell of a place.

Tulips

Forgiveness | dif - fi - cult |
act:

- the choice to release anger, fear and resentment for one's own mental, emotional and spiritual well being
- releasing expectations in preparation for recovery

Tulips

Justice

That mid of night drowned me in waving thoughts
and scars that left me itching to my notions
Like stockings seducing prickly legs hoping
for a scratching rub that dissolves what haunts them most

Drifting and floating in a stream of Epsom salts,
spring water, lavender and jasmine flowers revealed my faults
My own raveling must have come from a fountain cemented
with clay on a day where the winds left it dented

I have searched with aching arms for a passion
that seeps through every wrinkle of my skin
I took a leap of unorthodox faith and found within
what I have yearned for in the eyes of wounded sheep

That night where the stars stared through my window
I was led to the window of my soul
I was leveled with chocolate pupils that glow
holding scars scouring and screaming for recognition
Justice tilted her head encouraging a vision
of a future that promised me wings of fire and gold

Those wintered summers ring louder than the calling
of a wounded fowl and growl of a city falling
I crawled to the holy one who hears my pleas
to be released of those burning blades of my memories
Justice wearing red and crowned carried me to my throne
where I had seen that my tears were caused by the damage

of my own
beliefs of who I should have been to those women and men

Justice sat in the pits of my heart and burned when time was up
My detriments, afflictions, traumas and torments were cut
Sliced because she knew with her logic that I am worthy of love.

Forgiving with Reason

I no longer choose to be
a slave to past memories
What matters is the moment
in which I breathe
I choose to discover peace
intertwined within me

I hold dear the philosophy
that teaches me
reason and rationality
Compassion and magick are also
a part of my mystery
For they have healed my misery

KaSandra Turner

Dear body,

You have kept me alive for twenty-seven years. You consoled me during my emptiest times. You viewed me as a soul deserving of a thriving life despite my desolation. You humbly accepted the trash I consumed for nourishment and you performed as if you were tuned and polished. When I whipped you with my burning tongue, you humbled your spirit and your patience grew. While amid my solitude, during those nights I cried to the stars, you comforted me. I hadn't even realized. We nearly met our demise the time we were sick with the flu. I thought I had perished and to my surprise, I was met with another sunrise. You continued loving me as if I was You continued loving me as I was your God. When life formed within me, you stretched to make a comfortable space for that seed who grew to seven pounds and thirteen ounces. You healed quickly after all those slices and bruises the white coats gifted you. You nourished that seed despite how bruised and hurt you were. You have been my protector for the past twenty-seven years. You've been whipped and you shine as if not a single thread of leather slapped your surface. Even when I ignored you at times you saw my potential and waited patiently. When I stepped on you with filthy shoes like my neighbors had done, you remained still and vibrant. What a shame that I hadn't even noticed. I sit here with regretful eyes as they thunder and storm regret. As I write this letter you hold me with the warmth of your love and compassion . You remind me that:
I am beautiful.
I am healthy.
I am worthy.
I am love.

Tulips

Thank you for being the shell that houses my soul. I love you.

Growth

I morphed into a Sequoia tree
when I learned to release
expectations of others
My feathers fluttered far away
from those seeing my empathy
as brittle

Healing Through Forgiveness

Does forgiveness dry the rain
that flood through the walls
of our wounds?
Does forgiveness mend the cringing cries
that travel through the abyss of minds?
Does forgiveness reveal the strength
of armored hearts who fight to be whole?

I have subjective answers to these
However, through my tragedies
I have learned that forgiveness
is not for them,
but for me.

KaSandra Turner

We have the capacity for compassion
Yet, we still choose to be bitter
They say that compassion
makes us weak and soft
Perhaps we just haven't realized
that to be bitter is to be weak
Rational is what I choose to be.

Tulips

Loyalty

I plucked that lily
Even through her aching pain
She bowed before me

KaSandra Turner

Choosing to be Better

I too have ripped roots from the ground
I too have spit thorns
at those deserving and those not
Although this was during my immature days
the excuse is not mine to make

Instead I choose to help those
learn from my mistakes
I choose to be a tool for the future
I choose to be better
than I was yesterday

Tulips

When you see them
and can be in their presence without fear
When you can look at them
without the need to tear their ribs apart
When you're near them
and your stomach refuses to knot with
disgust, you did what they couldn't
You grew.

I Understand

Imagine not remembering your mother's smile
Imagine not knowing or feeling
your father and his sandpaper skin on your cheeks
Can you picture it?
Being oblivious to his name and face?
Imagine giving birth at seventeen
and teaching yourself to grow and mature
with fragments of lost faith and hope
haunting and hindering you from growth

I choose to understand this pain
Although I have my own strains
and wounds to patch,
I know that survival was her goal
She did what she felt would keep us alive
Now it's my turn
I'll teach her to thrive.

Tulips

Light the Shadows

We birth the demons
Tormented in our shadows
They yearn to be loved

A Monster's Motive

A monster's motive is never to scare
Its nails don't claw to taste your blood
Their screams are not to rape your ears
Their fur is not black to blend with night.

They scream because they are scared
They reach for you to hold them
They desperately crave your attention
They are black because you refuse to see them.

You see, monsters exist as the fires we reject
They are birthed from the fear of being true to ourselves
If only we would listen with our minds
and listen without fear

We would come to know that they aren't monsters,
but our shadows yearning to be seen
Shine the lights upon them!
They need releasing.

Archives of Honesty

I've lied as a child
to keep the trouble at bay
Dishonest as a teenager
to keep the judgement away
deep beneath the catacombs of bones

Fear was the foundation
of my dishonesty
And honestly,
that part of me
has withered to ashes
I will never again sacrifice
honesty for comfort

KaSandra Turner

Rainbows and Pretty Flowers

One thing I love
       about stormy days
              is that a rainbow

will find its way
       dancing down
              raging clouds

    The way it soothes
           that vengeful thunder
                singing life into
                      abandoned things

brings life everlasting,
       and poppies and tulips
              right into the palms
                      of my dreams

Tulips

My Dearest,

It was during those times where you bruised my skin and left me to heal in an ocean of crying sheets. I longed for your understanding and patience, but my ignorance demanded a seat beneath the window of your tolerance. You knew no better. For survival and the ghosts of your innocence whispered chants to you that were carried by your mothers. It is through your reflection that you sculpted me into a mold that mirrored your own afflictions. Perhaps I was the holy cloth soaking in your raging rivers of distress waiting to be led ashore. Why was I not more? Did I not deserve to eat the fruit of your guidance during those times? I longed to be vulnerable with you, but I was forced to dance in the depths of our fears instead. My upbringing exposed your deepest torments and afflictions, yet you covered them by convincing me that you only wanted me to live my highest best. This was only half truth, however. You needed an outlet for your cries. You wanted to be heard, felt, understood, seen and validated. You validated your wounds and masked your faults by convincing me that my perception of your actions was warped and exaggerated. I tried many times to express my fears to your crying heart, yet it only seemed to draw you further into your own sea of bones. It would be foolish of me to deny the times you tried your hardest to see with reason. There were days you shocked me by simply listening. Giving you chances was like flipping coins for life or death. Life because I could see the light of your potential. Your passion for us to succeed. Death because each time you scorned, screamed and physically hurt me you dissolved a part of my life force.

I have grown to realize that it is your spirit that is wounded. Your soul is fighting to shine through, yet the shadows that reside in you have too much power and control. I spent many moments hating our family for what they had done. Not just because you passed down these hurts to my spine, but because you were simply hurting.

Because you needed our blood relatives and everywhere you turned no one else was there. Even I made you feel as though I hated you. A part of me did. Yet, someone had to break the chain.

Because you know nothing of you, I now accept the duty to voyage to the land of my own truth. My truth as a woman. This truth will melt the chains that have bound me to your despair. In this truth, I will be freed. I will bask in the light of my newfound power and shower in the abundance of my gratitude. My knees will tremble with the fires of my accomplishments. My eyes will rain and storm with joy. My heart will soar through the cosmos with fulfillment.

My dearest, I hope to find you there in that land waiting for me with arms spread across the horizon, healed by the sun as he defrosts the ice beneath your rib cage. Will you be there waiting for me? Should I not find you there healed and vulnerable, I will rejoice for you. It is through my songs of freedom that this curse will be lifted. That, my love is truth. I love you.

-Your Reflection

Tulips

She was bathed in anomalies by those who taught her that she was unworthy. Her confidence was a joke because to them she was better off an outcast. In her seclusion, she discovered that her beauty is infinite in every direction; it could never be destroyed.

They now bow to her wisdom and regret the days they deemed her unworthy. She is their mother, and they look to her for guidance. She guides them because they now seek salvation. She forgave them and their hearts were moved.

-She is God.

You hid your bump underneath your shirts and jeans. When they found your secret, they tried convincing you I'd ruin your life. They told you to abort the mission.

You birthed me in your teenage years because you refused to sacrifice the most precious thing God had ever given you. Despite the changes your body had gone through, you made it work the best way you could.

I sit and simmer in the thoughts of our times of laughter. Your pranks on Halloween left me screaming and laughing after. My heart sizzles when I drench in the memories of your kool-aid smiles after the dinners we devoured when you slaved the day away.

Despite the comfort that loneliness bestowed upon your heart, you mothered me the best way you knew how. You laughed and slaved through some of your pain singlehandedly. How could I not honor that fact?

Tulips

They did the best they could, but it wasn't enough.
It wasn't enough, but they did the best they could.
Despite how we choose to perceive this, everyone is
trying to survive. I simply wish for *all* of us to *thrive.*

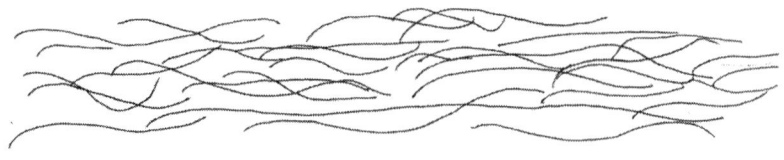

KaSandra Turner

Let's Have a Chat

I think I'm ready for that conversation
        You know,
the one where we discuss how our parents
find it disrespectful
if we plea our feelings in desperation
        You know,
The talk that reveals our ignored feelings
and their suppressed traumas.

I think I'm ready for that conversation
        You know,
the one where we hold our parents
responsible for their actions
        You know,
the conversation where we refuse to let
them remain anchored in their perception
blinded by a victim mentality

I think I'm ready for that conversation
        You know,
The one where we listen to their secrets
acknowledge their stories
and hug them tightly
        You know,
The one where we call upon our ancestors
sit at our parents' feet
while they cry out their pain

I think I'm ready for that conversation

Tulips

      You know,
the one where we fearlessly release
these generational burdens
and integrate new ideas
in traditional values

I'm ready to listen
I'm ready to speak up
and I'm ready for this healing
because this trauma, you see
it ends with me.

Your eyes shine brighter than they have in years.
Your lips reveal a blazing, laughing tongue as if pain never touched your skin. Your spirit is a field of star gazing sunflowers. Having your grandchild brought angels to the earth and I can tell that heaven is with you every time he smiles at you.

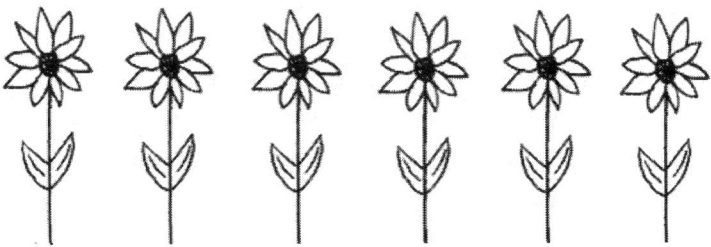

Tulips

Although you have scars
in places I've never been,
we are waters of the same well.
I can tell
by the ringing of your voice
how proud you are of your sprout
who grew from seed.

-A Father's daughter

KaSandra Turner

Ten of Swords

What makes me forgive you is
the fact that your traumas
are recycled in your blood
 You lived your life unaware
of the power that our ancestors
bestowed upon your wings.
To live a life without a mother
and a father
with no memories of them must be
like sleeping on knives and needles
pointing right into your chest and dreams.

I promise that one day
the clouds will dance away,
the sun will stretch his rays,
and dry away your rain.
You did what you thought was best
Now leave your swords to rest
I'll take it from here,
rest now.

Jasmines

Recovery | heal - ing |
process:

- a period in which one submerges in the rivers of their own unconditional love and understanding in preparation for their transformation
- a baptism

Jasmines

Let your tears flow, love. Scream until the walls bleed. Purge the toxins you consumed during your youth until now. Fall to your knees at the altar of your mercy. Your upbringing is not your fault.

You are not a blanket that shelters their traumas. Healing is arduous, raw, and necessary. Your time for recovery is now.

-Chiron

KaSandra Turner

To the one with their chest to their knees
arms locked around their legs
approaching their demise
in the abyss of oblivion

To the one who's eyes
caress the palms of their hands
while their spine slithers and sweats
against that freezing wall

To the one who howls and prays
to the blood moon for a taste
of relief with a throat dryer
than raisin lips in a summer desert

I swim in the sea of your fears
You are the mirror exposing
my deepest impurities
We are perfect reflections.

-I see you

Jasmines

Healing forces you to be vulnerable,
completely naked, and exposed.
That's how the cleansing starts.

KaSandra Turner

I casted spells to purge my burdens.
Thoughts of them sliced through my chest and
fled through my window.
Their chains cackled behind them.
It's only the beginning.

    -Dragon's Blood

Jasmines

Prayer to My Higher Self

Take me as I am
bruised, torn and withered
I lay my detriments
on the altar of your grace
Divine, I thank you
for your trickles of tender kisses
in those screeching seconds and minutes
of the ripping pain

You cracked me open
wide like the split sea
revealing what needed
to be pured within me
Thank you for the promise
of life after death
Thank you for the strength
for another breath

KaSandra Turner

Flowers for Dreams

Jasmines and lilies
Their sweet singing scents afar
Send love to my dreams

Footprints

My soles breathe prints
in the soil of my desires
leaving ash from the fires
that hint my whereto
They seek to follow
my path and fail
Their thin skins last not
in the pits of my hells

They fail to see
that those before me,
left feathers for my findings
amid their prints
No step was made
or danced in vanity
Like them I too leave prints
as I journey to sanity.

Midnight Prayer

Tear my torso into an open half
Reveal the nakedness
of life unclenched
Sing your essence into my sack
Oh Divine, see me more
than for what I lack

Cave Crystals and Natural Things

I ache to travel through the darkest of caves
to feel the energy
of crystals never seen
I'd rather dwell in the depths of their shine
than to worry in a world
that wouldn't waste a second
to destroy what's mine
My eyes sprinkle in satisfaction
of the sparkling stars
surfacing the skies in scatter pieces
They'd rather lay
on the skin of the heavens
than to sink into seductions of lies
I'd prefer my nose be filled with clover,
basil and limes
than the breath of faint fires
of puny passions
I ache to feel dense dirt and soil
rub between my fingers
as the sour scent of lemongrass
lingers through my nostrils
I yearn to listen to the winds
tell the truths of tribes
who danced to bring the rain
and sang together beside
wolves, deer and turtles
wearing feathers and buffalo hide
I'd prefer the salty smell of the ocean

KaSandra Turner

fill my breath
as she sneaks onto the shore
and tickles my toes
while protecting the secrets
of what dwells below
I'd rather smirk at the sand
as she sparkles and holds
turtle eggs and seashells
It is in that womb, that garden
that I'd prefer to converse
with prancing pansies
than panic in the pulsing presence
of mirrorless saints
tainted in tarred sins.

Jasmines

Some days you feel like you've climbed to the highest cloud and kissed the sun's forehead. Some days you feel like you're drowning, wondering when it will all end. It doesn't make any sense.

That's because you're actually doing it. You're healing at your own pace. You're doing it your way.

KaSandra Turner

Intuitive Mother

I remember gazing through the cracks
of ground stapled with green blades
and puffy white flowers with yellow buds
The war of winds cut through my blackened knees
as I stayed out past streetlight hours
and showered in the laughter of those happy stars
The pregnant moon followed me as I pranced
and ran atop that earthy lawn
wondering why she followed me
I often wondered why I would find her there
changing, losing and gaining
her light on different days in the darkest of nights

What did she feel that I could hardly fathom
during the days I could faintly describe
the reason for the bleeding between a woman's thighs?
I remember one crispy night in October I cried
whined and whimpered wanting to meet those dips
and dark spots of that celestial body
Anywhere was better than existing in the experience
of the crippling burn through my veins in a world
that gifted pain to clays that weren't tan
and pretty like rose flowers

The only ones I felt loved me with a dragon's passion
were those stars and that motherly light because
without fail she followed and watched over me
She kissed me to sleep and made sure
I dreamt dreams f dolphins dolls and fairies

Jasmines

She faithfully peeked through my window
on the nights I wished I wasn't breathing
She kept my heart beating
So that I may write this poem for you to read
and know that she loves you too,
without condition.

KaSandra Turner

The Way Back

I'll build a bridge from the bones of me
I'll lay them across the sea,
in hopes that you'll see
the way back to you.

I'll stretch my spine along a waterfall
Toes to the sky, head below
in hopes that you'll know,
a safe way to you.

I'll shiver and shatter my essence for us
My pieces starring the skies
in hopes that you'll find,
the way back to you.

When your fingertips fade far into the shore
and your knees dance with the trees,
my eyes will sing in glee
because you have found
the way back to you.

She is Strength

She carries mountains on her fingertips
The skies look up to her guidance
She sways the waters with the tips of her hips
Volcanoes simmer at her silence
Minds bleed at the speed of her wits
as eyes pause at the shine of her teeth
She creates lands of infinite bliss
as her feet shatters worlds beneath
She holds the world in her womb
as her arms stretch across the horizon
And even when she cries
She still cannot be moved
She is no ordinary woman
She is strength

KaSandra Turner

If you crave solitude
go out into nature
Listen to the birds sing
Watch the leaves on the trees
wave in the wind
Watch the waters glisten
as the sun kisses his reflection
Observe the rainbows
on the back of your eyelids
Breathe deeply and slowly
Be still in the present moment
Let your tears, fears, and stress evaporate
while you sink into Mama Earth.

-Get grounded

Jasmines

Indigenous Music

Wooden rattle snakes
Turtle shells and hallow gourds
Is my kind of vibe

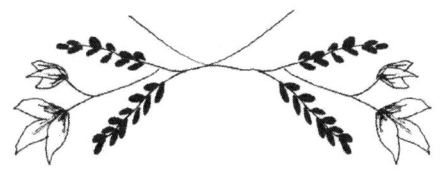

Daily Mantra

I am in tune with my essence
I am rooted in passion
I am wise with love
I am expressive of my desires
I am safe in abundance
I am one with the universe
I am still
I am soothed
I am peace

Jasmines

Self-care isn't always vibrant red roses tickling pillows and sheets on a hotel's bed with the stranger you met last week. It isn't always that perfect snapshot of a coffee mug angled next to an unopened book behind a vintage filter. Appreciating yourself is not an illusion of your life's happiest moments in photos with thousands of approval points.

Self-care is submitting to the reflection who exposes demons buried beneath screaming streams. Self-care is reminding yourself that even though your shoes have hitch hiked through realms of disaster, that your survival is a first-place gold medal.

Self-love is accepting the parts of yourself who you beat and tortured to please the souls of those with insecurities just like you. It is understanding your soul's worth to a God's degree. It requires permission from no one, but the creator, which is you.

Self-love is rejection and acceptance.

-Message from a seasoned soul

Those flower vines across your belly are beautiful.
The way they tickle your womb is so divine!

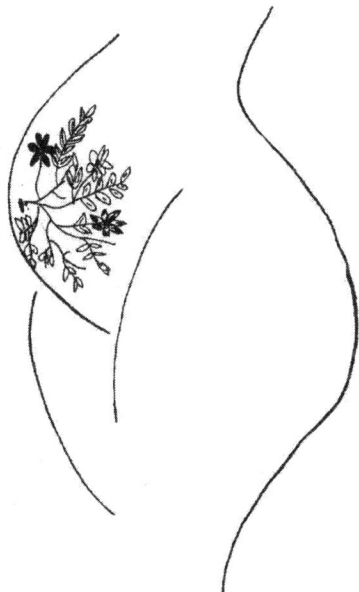

Jasmines

Sunday's Note

I often weep and wonder how this all came to be
When will I discover why this all happened to me?
Shown no love as an ignorant youth
I have grown so tired indeed, a loose tooth.
An outcast to those that I fail to be
Whipped to the ground and forced to my knees
Stripped bare to reveal my insecurities
displayed on a screen for their comedy
They laughed and they danced at the site of me
and left me to sit alone under a tree
I'm starting to believe
that this life was meant for me
I am so undeserving of love indeed.

On a fine Sunday, when the sun seduced my skin
I was pleased to find a note down from deep within:
Look at those curls as they reach for the sun
Watch them dance, sing and play
one by one
Your feet strut and shake the ground
revealing a path untouched and unbound
The sway of your hips
the perk of those lips
that beautiful chin
and that rich chocolate skin
Get a good sniff of that succulent scent
of coconuts, berries, sage and mint

KaSandra Turner

You are one of nature's finest
don't you dare forget!
Remember these words or else you'll regret
Those others are reflections of what needs to heal
and when they meet you
their insecurities you reveal.

So, light that incense!
Burn that sage!
Ground yourself and turn that page
You embody beauty indeed
In mind, in spirit, and physically
Remember these words on this Sunday
You are everything baby girl,
Asé!

Jasmines

She offered her heart as a journal to help heal the world. Yet, they only wrote stories of hate and burned her pages. The ashes of their stories remain.

They failed to know that she was born of fire.
Her passion is infinite.
So is her desire to heal...

KaSandra Turner

Sleeping Sun

The smiling sun sets
Bowing to my brown lit skin
He kissed me and slept

Jasmines

All You Need

You are all you need
to find your happy place
You are all you need
to wrap your arms around peace
You are capable, strong,
beautiful, and irreplaceable
Don't you dare think twice
about your worth
When you heal yourself
you heal your mothers and fathers
before you
That is magic, my love
You are magic!

KaSandra Turner

Breathe

The green leaves blowing
Caressing the clouds and wind
Remind me to breathe

Jasmines

The universe
with its all-knowing heart
will pour gold into souls
that shine with gratitude
Those bouncing, beaming, cosmic lights
scattered so flawlessly
reveal the true beauty
we prize and possess

If we properly used our egos
as the tools that they are
we would discover
the universe within us.

KaSandra Turner

Mother

Her hair is abundant
as it reaches for the stars
Her skin blends with the night
as it dances against the clouds
Her heart paints the skies
as trees bow to her kindness.

Her womb holds generations
so that she can birth the future
How can we not love her?
She is mother

Jasmines

We Need You, Mother

Look at that reaching mountain
far off in the distance
See how its points caress the clouds?
Look at that sparkling dust
scattered above
See how it dances and sings aloud?

You are that mountain and sparkling dust
Without you the world is unjust
Your womb can hold two generations
at once
We need you mother
For we are birthed from your love

KaSandra Turner

I sat still and silenced and slowly breathed
life into myself before a tarot reading
I decided to gift myself the same energy
I had poured into other fountains
I decided I was worthy enough to be
acknowledged, by myself at least
I shuffled those cards, gently
They popped out in excitement
My guides were speaking

When I peered through those cards
a revelation revealed itself
I sobbed.
I mourned.
I screamed.
Then, a weight lifted
It fled from me
I laid on my side
as the screams became laughs
For the first time in years
I breathed.

How We Heal

When I mend the bend of my stems
hers too, come close to mine
When my petals mettle in the wind
hers too, become divine
When my leaves tickle the toes of skies
hers too, shall dance in grace
When my garden gleams that peaceful prize
she will bask in that happy place
When I exhale the cries that haunt my past
she too, shall breathe relief
When I shut the eyes of that tortured mass
she too, shall be at peace
To the queens who live and skip through me
You are favored and loved indeed.

KaSandra Turner

Their tongues ache for redemption
as the sting of their burdens
burn ice cold cracks
around the skin of their dying hearts.
Salvation was once her enemy,
but clarity now colors the breast
of her sanity

I'm Ready

I remember the times when fear would comfort me
during those daunting moments
I sat surrounded by a whirlpool of wondering whispers hoping
to be lifted from this storm of haunting bones choking
the last breath out of me
I would whisper in my mind
curses of grieving rhymes
vehemently

Believe me, these were the days
I declared myself a waste of walking flesh
I guess I was naïve to think
that I was purposeless
I scorned myself to death
because my perception of life was shattered
Fragments of hope left me drowning, beaten and battered
I remained meek because I believed in the potential
of their grandeur purpose
The silhouettes of their power rang loud against my fragility

I reflect on these memories ever so often
I express my gratuity to my guides because they softened
my shell after collapsing me open
I was sentient, yet remained unconscious of my power
I was a slave to my transgressions and was constantly devoured

KaSandra Turner

I can now stare at these memories in confidence
I have made peace with these parts of me
and that is how I know
that I am ready to take on the world
FEARLESSLY.

Lotus

Transformation | re-birth |
process:
- transmuting traumas into treasures to help heal the world
- enlightenment

Lotus

My strength emerged
when I stepped into my divinity
and reclaimed
my rightful place
as Queen

She is Eden

She has discovered the soil
that grounds her roots
and nourishes her soul
She has found the garden
watered by her tears
Her waterfalls of fears
stream into this scape of green,
raging then still

With her many flowers
of violet, lavender, lilac
and many
None is plucked
because she now knows love
since she discovered
that she is Eden.

Lotus

To be led by fire is foolish
To stay sunk in soil is limiting
But to be grounded in passion?
What a perfect way
to ignite your dreams.

The Love She Truly Is

Without eyes she saw
Without skin she felt
Without feet she walked
Without hate she dwelt
Without hands she healed
For her heart revealed,
the love she truly is.

Lotus

I am Eden

You dug into my soil
with stained hands
You discovered reaching roots
choked my stems
and ripped them from Earth
Even she cried in pain
You plucked my roots
one by one and tossed me

What you didn't know
was that Mama Earth
would bury me into her womb
scatter my seeds
use my tears to water me
use my rage and passion to warm me

With her love and gentle care
I was reborn
Call me by my name!

KaSandra Turner

The More You Know

We often pause in awe to observe a flower's petals
We say, *wow! look how beautiful these daisies are!*
Some may even pluck them.

We will stretch our necks up to a Hyperion
and marvel at its height
We gasp for life at the sight of its trunk.

How often do we think of how they came to be?
How often do we think of their roots,
their seeds?

To truly know a flower or a tree
one must know its roots
and how it grew into its beauty.

Resurrected

You buried me as my breath raced for life
You submerged me in the soil of my own garden
You failed to realize
that you completed the ritual
needed for my cleansing

I am no longer a slave to you
I speak for the Queens
and High Priestesses before me
I hold our crowns within my crown
At our love and magick, you will bow!

KaSandra Turner

Haiku of God

When I searched for God
I bathed in holy waters
I am that I am

Lotus

I sometimes find myself captivated by the nakedness revealed in the cosmos. It feels so familiar, staring into these twinkling lights. It's as if I'm peering through my own nakedness. Through the raw and unfiltered me. The brightest light leads me to my destiny. But really, it's just me guiding me.

KaSandra Turner

For the first time in eons
I finally found the fierceness
to stare into my soul
through a recognized portal
I sense a familiarity
in this aura
Like brain cells mirrored
in the cosmos
like stardust revealing
its patterns in my cells

I'm baffled at the fact
that it took me this long
to find this place
when all I had to do
was close my eyes and breathe
With this sacred breath
being carried to God
I'll set my intention
and prepare for rebirth

Autumn Equinox

The quaking of new beaming being
warms my stomach
like cinnamon tea steaming
brewed with creamy oat milk and spices
sipped on a cold crisp night
full with the moon's delight
Death in leaves
crunch with tangy orange bodies
brittle with bright brown skins
fall to meet the cement's surface

Harvesting and savoring
life's abundance
with gleaming gratitude subdues
my fears of lack
and prepares my soul
for death and rest
Intentions written on kraft brown paper
burned in a womb
smoke and spiral above
are preserved
and wait to emerge
to fruit in May and June

Cheers to those howling winds
screaming against burgundy bricks
Ode to that cackling, fuzzy fire
that exposes the dancing and stomps
of my ancestors who dwelt
as chiefs and oracles

KaSandra Turner

Spicy cinnamon sweats on my lips
as I cheer to the good life of harvest
as I prepare to perish
and transform.

Waving Willows

Why do willows wave their wands
in whispering winds flying in moonlight?
It seems as though they know
their slowly swaying hips of vines
seduce my soul into a trance
despite their lack of eyes.

How is it that they know
the pulsing path behind my knees
despite the marvelous muck of mud
protecting my occult memories?

I suppose that when they gaze and grow
wise and transform in waves of time
they feel and see all things
as a collection of thoughts and dreams.

KaSandra Turner

Love Thyself

Loving all of you
So deeply, so intensely
Will help heal your world

My Sweet Majestic

When the stars dance in the midst of twilight
When the waters' rays kiss the full moon's chin
When the swallows leap and wings take flight
Your soul turns men's anger to grins
As the soil splits paths for each beat of your feet
The grapes of vines you will forevermore reap
You are true to the dreams of thieves
Your leaves they wish to pluck and receive
The juice of your fruit they yearn to taste
As each peach grows, none replaced
Your jewels twin the light of the sun
As they gaze into your eyes and meet
Eternal thoughts intertwined in one
How majestic you are, my sweet, sweet love

KaSandra Turner

*I won't drown in the rushing rivers of guilt
for not embracing my essence
Instead I'll stay rooted in every moment
breathing in prana
reaching nirvana
I'll drink from a fountain of reverence
to keep my vessel full and well nourished
with divine love
poured directly from source*

You Chose Love

You allowed your heart to soften
like cotton candied clouds
on a sunny day
despite the ball of nails
they threw at you
It amazes me
how graceful and fearless you are
How your determination
rests proudly on your shoulders
like a towel on a heavyweight
I am thrilled to know
that you found it
in your best interest
to pick up your pieces
and theirs too
You remembered your power
and avoided the bittersweet taste of revenge
like a poisoned plague

I am a proud observer
of the way you have moved
to let yourself love
and be loved
You had nothing to prove
yet, you proved
that the frequency of love
ocannot only be felt,
but seen.

KaSandra Turner

You are the portal
that leads souls from the
cosmos into this dream
Your streams of golden nectar
give life and strength
to those who grow ten feet

You teach,
you nurture,
you grow
How could they not know your
name?

-Divine Feminine

Lotus

Her intention is to share her light and magick with the world. Her deepest desire is to heal herself and those around her. She effortlessly embodies grace and wisdom blessed by the wounds and torments during those days she scavenged for her sanity. She knows her power and inner stands the meaning of sacrifice.

She welcomes birth and destruction, for these cycles are sacred to her and have revealed the magnitude of her strength. It is fear who fears her courage and blessings. There is nothing unknown to her despite her obscurity. She trusts the Divine, seeks guidance from her ancestors and paces intentionally with intuition. Her fingers turn roots to gold; there is nothing her heart cannot heal and uphold. She co-creates her reality with focused intention because the veil no longer stings her eyes. Her clarity enlightens the souls around her as she speaks with closed lips and tingling ears.

She is the future, the past and the present.
She is what the world needs.

-Goddess Vibes

Sisterhood

If your breath wreaks of envy
and skin crawls with grotesque
at another woman's ways
ask yourself,
is it her that I hate?
Or do I see in her
what I lack in me?
Before you trample
on your sister's shortcomings
and cackle at her tears
ask yourself,
does she embody my shed skin?
Or have I not fully healed
these aspects of me?
Have I found pleasure
in piercing crawling knees?

We all embody the divine feminine
We form seas as a unit
and these waters emulate
our divine essence
If only we would wrap our wounds
with wisdom
form chains and chant spells
that speak life into our roots
We would come to know
that the sisterhood

Lotus

is not just what we
have, but who we *are*.

How miserable I was to seek self-awareness through sewn eyes. How foolish of me to pace my journey on another's feet. Why did I choose to dwell in an Eden other than the one most sacred to me? I have shattered into infinite pieces just to find my way back to peace. I failed to realize my power, my potential and searched for my star in the light of others. How undoubtedly desperate and dim my beam chose to be. I trained myself to seek symbols that validated my lack of self-acceptance. I trained myself to submit to the whips of blind beasts who reek of belligerent feasts. I chose to be guided by entities with eyes like me.

It was at that moment of my final plea when my heart stormed screams and prayed for signs. Signs that validated my afflictions conceived in the womb of my insecurities. When my eyes met gaze with strength, coins and that Virgo moon I discovered the power of wholeness. I discovered the most complex yet simple truth that clenched the pits of my soul: there is strength in letting go. You ARE good enough. Surrender to your compassion.

I refuse to allow another energy to claw and infect my spirit with toxic nails again. I am a pulsing torch whose flame orgasms with precise intention. I will flame and fly across the cosmos beside that shooting star on a twinkling summer night. I AM that shooting star.

Empress Energy

She is the queen of all things
sacred and pure
She extends her love
to every soul birthed
by Mother Earth
Every creed of rock,
every spine of the seas,
and every waving tree
knows her
as they know them
She surrenders to the Divine
Her body, and spirit and mind
trine and receive blessings abundantly
And her beauty, oh my
reflects the radiance of her soul
Her womb gleams with things renewed
She is the mother of birth herself
How mighty, how graceful and gentle she
is That beautiful Empress
Even the heavens form
singing songs of her love.

Whose permission do you need when it comes to manifesting your desires? Who calls the shots on what you need to have a fulfilling life? Who approves what visions you manifest for yourself to ensure your evolution and adaptability? We sometimes think that being validated in some ways means that we're doing it right. However, what happens when we don't get the validation we're searching for? Do we continue down that path or change course because someone disagreed with what we intuitively felt was right?

One of the things that makes us sexy is knowing what we want without the fear of declaring it as ours. See the vision. Feel the vision. Be the vision. Work your magick. It is an expression of yourself as a creator and an enlightened being.

Be you. Be sexy. Be wild.

ALWAYS.

Lotus

Remember that moment in your recovery where nothing and everything made sense?
Remember how your traumas were abstract?
It's profound that now they all make perfect sense.
It was excruciating, but you made it.
You *made* it...

I never understood my undying love for other people. I often cried to my pillows because I was convinced that people weren't aware of my presence and significance. I felt they didn't understand me with the same love and intensity.

I was distraught because I felt that my traumas and fears were a burden to others. As horribly as people treated me, I still had the urge to help them. To heal them. To love them. I *still* have this passion.

As long as oxygen flows through my lungs and I have a way to speak, I will continue extending my petals to other flowers. This gift is rare and I will share it. Forever.

-Moldavite

Lotus

Rising Phoenix

Even the phoenix
Rises from the burning ash
With wisdom and strength

To have a cup filled with expectation and attachment is suicide. I've killed myself a billion times waiting for deep intimacy. When I peered inwards, all I needed was there coiled at the base of my spine.

I will never expect anyone else to have a torch like me. To flow with my currents. To dive deep into my shadows and seas. I'll never expect anyone to vibe like me. When I embraced and integrated this simple wisdom, life slithered up my spine. I'll forever be awakened.

Lotus

Loving Them is not Enough

Love is not always about attachment,
for detachment is how flowers bloom
Their seeds don't stay in that bud
always The breeze, bees and birds
carry them to be buried in soil
When they sprout and petals stretch
their seeds are dispersed again.

Birds nest with their eggs
beneath them to give warmth
They rise bright and early
to feed their hatchlings
When those babies flap their wings,
age and sore through the skies
to that nest they will never return
For they have learned to fly.

Love those dear to you
with grace and intuition,
with nurturing hands
and a strong mind
Love yourself so deeply,
that you allow them room to grow
and breathe
Love yourself so unconditionally,
that you'll smile when they leave.

Tribute to Ancestors

You welcomed these men
into your love and care
You taught them of the sacred
rhythms gifted by Earth Mother

They thanked you by conforming you
to false ideologies of God
and stripped your freedom
raped our women
and tortured our men

Your blood boils through my veins
passionately, patiently, persistently
in faith that I'll lift this curse
this generational pain.

Now that I know
my worth, my roots, my strength
I will never stop fighting
never stop loving
and never stop healing
I owe it all to you.

Lotus

The Divine has shown us time and time again
that our evolution is destined
despite our yearn for comfort
We often find the root, the strength of our
strengths during tumultuous times
Each day we choose to pace in truth
we expose an unseen vibrancy
that will be perceived by the ready,
the intuitive,
the warriors
When you walk in your truth
and speak with a tongue of precision you'll be
a leader amongst leaders
You have earned your crown.

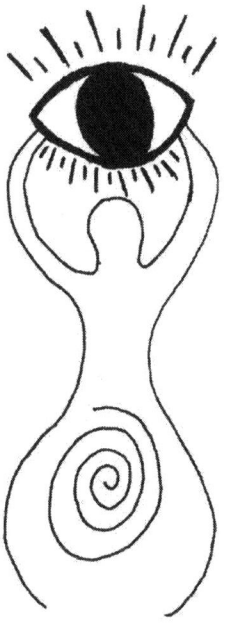

Embracing the depths of your abyss
is an act of self-love and an expression
of the divine feminine.

Feminine Power

They won't see you coming,
but they'll feel you
They won't see you running,
but they'll hear you
And when you strike
that sword with might,
they'll fear you

Can you imagine?
An army of goddesses
reclaiming their worlds?
That is what they fear
Stand together!

Let's Show Up!

Let's show up in our skin
deepest of deep, dark and shining
light as light and golden agave
with our shades shading
the mass of our globe
with our stripes scattered
across our wombs
so sexy and succulent

Let's show up in our skin
bottom thick and top heavy
slim, skinny and love handled
with braids below the lows of our knees
our straight and curly hair
flowering and stemming from different worlds
with fros defying the demands of gravity
eyes revealing tribes indigenous to lands
with glory and pride

Let's show up in our skin
act up and show out
dance together in laughter
in all of our visions of beauty
Let's show the masses our truth
and our scars
Let's write our stories
in the stars
We are more than beauty
Divine is what we are!

Lotus

I am not a half of light
I am not a half of night
I am the perfect whole of both
See me with your eye

KaSandra Turner

Love Your Demons

I found the courage to gaze upon my demons
I discovered familiar eyes
I found that they were the parts of my depths
left undiscovered
Now I cannot dream
of a life without them.

Even if I dared to wish them away
they'll remain there lurking
If integrate them proudly,
even give them names
I'll learn to rise above them
and they'll be fulfilled
eternally.

Lotus

Let Us Return Home

There is so much beauty
infinitely expressed through unlimited fractals
that construct our universe
They all dance uniquely
birthing the heavens and earth
Each moment of our lives
is but one of these fractals
that merge and blend into one another
forming a web that reveals our stories
Our lives weave into another's
creating this dream world
of space and time

I suppose that if we follow our vibes
intuitively and give reverence to others
we'd finally evolve
and all return home
Although I won't see this in my lifetime,
I'll plant these seeds in my children
in hopes that they'll trickle down
into the deepest parts of their minds
I'll spread my message
in hopes that it will be carried
and held in the hearts of the world
so that we'll all evolve together
and return home.

KaSandra Turner

"Let thyself unfold.
Go and share thy gifts upon the multitudes
like the many flowers of abundance.
They are divine expressions of wisdom.
And if ye are God,
as thy sisters and brethren,
let thyself be known as sacred."

-Book of Shadows Entry

Lotus

Last night I dreamt a familiar dream.
I dwelt in the truest realm.
Although there was no *I*, *we* were
there in our purest form
waltzing into creation
in the void.

Transformation

I dwell under a pixie dust sky and full moon around a campfire as it hisses chants and screams of the women before me. I sit there with the girls I have been and plea for the women I'm destined to be. We have the same branchy brown skin and thick curly hair, the color of midnight black.

Six years screams and cries for her mother to love her gently because her skin burns hotter than the campfire she's next to. Eleven and fifteen weep while their tears meet the dust beneath their feet. Eighteen years watches while fear chokes her with the chains of six year's screams. I run my fingers through her scalp and gently press her head upon my bosom. The rapid drumming through my chest pacifies her cheeks. I scoop six years and rock them both like newborn twins. We sweat there, numbed with eyes captivated by that dancing fire. Eighteen whispers, *will this river of torture ever stop flowing?* Silence swallows the wind and carries the sizzling burn as it glows through the whites of her eyes. We scry into that screaming campfire as slithering emerges from the willows north of us. Twenty-five reveals herself as she sheds her snake skin like a jacket on a melting summer day. She poses there, with eyes below the heavens and hands gripping the hips of her black, satin laced dress like a mountain climb. Her lips reveal, *you need this river to flow into the womb of your garden.*

In comes thirty-three and forty-four riding a silky midnight stallion whose dark coat reveals the full moon's kisses along her structure. They approach in silence, bare and vulnerable as their essence stills the fire. The pair of them dance giving thanks to the goddess who has seen the torment endured by us all. Their heads bob as sacred drums rattle and shake the skies. Their feet stomp revealing pebbles and prints of the elders who carry their souls atop the soil. They merge to one and prance around our sacredmspace. All my senses cease as my quivering hands extend towards the newly merged figure. Her fingers intertwine with mine. I reveal my pleading eyes to find them, me, swaying there around that now raging, chanting fire.

My ego is completely exposed, bare and fragile as it fights to lie inside my mushy sack while they anticipate my resurrection. Within the quiver of a lip, I am released of my ego's grip and sucked into the infinite waves of the void. This is the place where "I", "we", dwell in our purest form. Each of our traumas warp into bowing beings of submission and crawl to the gates of holy lights. Spectrums of infinite indigos, greens and geometric shapes merge and dance in pure love and bliss. Eager yellows and singing oranges hug each other in the most complex patterns indescribable by the human tongue. Eruptions of raging vibrations and warping thoughts seduce my soul sending it through infinite loops of orgasmic beams. Fear no longer exists as I surrender to that greater than "me". There is no pretending. Just the seducing sounds of crystalline fragments, sine and cosine waves waving across what is no longer left, right, up or down. This womb space of creation is all there is, all there was and all that ever will be. Creation is absolute. Creation is infinite. This is the truest of all dimensions. This place is the truest of all dimensions. This place is home.

I gasp for the familiar breath as my soul is slapped back into my body. My body moans as orgasmic epiphanies make love to my mind. *Your traumas are needed to warp the world. Every scream, every ounce of sorrow and every tear is but a color of thought.*

Each profound moment of joy, fulfillment and satisfaction are infinite clusters and counting. Live a life of freedom, for the universe does not create with limitation. We are the universe pacing on the feet of creation. Our shattering is the perfect act of peace and destruction. We are being led to the wings of infinity...

Each part of me stands there grouped together with tears of fulfillment as they hug forming a chain of sunflowers and roses. They approach me, bow with encouraged hearts and slowly fade into my body forming an unrecognizable essence. That beautiful pregnant moon kissed by the suns confidence nurtured me into my morphing. My soul has been exposed and my perception of life will forever be moved. I have found my calling.

You have made it to the end. Our hearts are one since we have discovered that we are flowers of the same garden. Your willingness to connect with me is a gift I will never take for granted. Thank you, Divine for opening your heart and allowing your spirit to fly alongside mine. I'll have you know that this journey isn't the end. Our journey is infinite. Allow me to take hold of your right hand as we sore to Magick of Eden.

A Note from Eden

Eden is a womb space that welcomes exiled souls who ache for recovery. It is a garden prized and ready for those who seek true enlightenment and knowledge of the self. Dwelling in this space is for those who choose to be led through the shadows by their own divine love and supreme intelligence. Truly, it is a representation of your intuitive knowing of who you are and what you need in order to unfold, reclaim your divinity and evolve. Although I am not defining Eden as a physical place, it absolutely *can* be. It can be any place that you declare as sacred. It can be an actual garden, an altar, and anywhere that you can be physically, spiritually and mentally nourished. It can be anywhere you are free to be vulnerable and comfortable in your most authentic light.

When I submerged myself in this womb, I was confronted by the shadows that consumed and led to me my own destruction. I was forced to burn in the fires fueled and forged by the powers of my anger, resentment, guilt and shame. This forced me to return to the most vulnerable and shattered parts of myself because I realized that I was not living a thriving life, but rather a life of fear and limitation. I wanted so desperately to be accepted by those who hardly knew their own potential. I whipped and burned my essence in attempts to match their flawed ideals of how a human should be.

My Eden was born the moment I accepted that I needed to break the chains of generational traumas that haunted the backbone and structure of my family. I realized at an early age that I allowed myself to be consumed by the beautiful flaws of other people's realities. I often felt as though this world was too small for me and that my dedication and love floated off into the void to be

KaSandra Turner

consumed and sucked into nothing. I have always had a yearn to connect and help people on an intensely deep, emotional and spiritual level. Hence why I thought that taking the psychological beatings of my family and the world was the ultimate sacrifice. What I have learned from accepting my calling as a truth seeker and healer is that everything outside of me is a pebble that leads me back to my roots and my light. Dwelling in this heaven revealed the magic and power that sat in the pits of my guts, like Justice who burned when time was up. Thorns were piercing lights of truth that shined upon the spines of my shadows. These shadows were formed from the rejected and the most unique and authentic parts of myself as a young woman. I was weakened and withered by those that I allowed to suck the pure life from my vessel. I sacrificed the most intimate parts of my being in hopes that I could help reshape this world. Even if it meant doing it alone. Each tulip and lily I plucked forgave me and showed me that the roots of forgiveness begin within the abyss of the self. I had to acknowledge my devils and accept the fact that they were birthed from my lack of integration, understanding, self-love and self-acceptance. I feared and rejected their existence. I failed to understand that to fear and hate them was to fear and hate myself. I had to forgive *me* for not trusting in my divine power. For plucking my roots along with those who despised and misunderstood me. Each jasmine that sang at night taught me how to breathe through the recovery process. Their beauty and radiance gave me comfort on the days and nights I stormed and screamed. The lotus. The one who emerged from the muck without ever being phased revealed itself when I was worthy of its presence. It showed me the magnificence of its aura at that perfect moment of completion. It revealed itself as mirrored aspect of me. This was indeed my higher self. This evolved version of me protected and sat with me through those moments I wanted to end my suffering. It spoke and radiated a frequency that eased the bruises that surfaced my skin. This divine light carried me to my calling. It led me to you.

Tribe, please remember that we are not limited or defined by our suffering. It is, however through these experiences that we can reclaim our power and become in sync with the creative and rational parts of ourselves. To become our highest selves, we must transmute our energy and project our wills into this shared dream world. This ensures that we are co-creating the reality we envision for ourselves. This is indeed an act of alchemy and magick.

For anyone struggling to find their place in the world please remember that you are a creator. Let your will be done. You are more than the surface of your skin. You are worthy of creation. Fear is sometimes the addiction that anchors and keeps us hindered from living our highest potential. At least this was true for me. Forgive yourself for searching for your soul through the mistakes of others. Embrace your shadows and allow your intellect to guide your emotions and intuition. You are a SUPREME being and everything you touch grows tenfold!

I am proud of you for having made it this far along your journey. However, I hope that when you stare into your eyes that you see someone worthy to be proud of. I hope that when you are faced with the growls of adversity that you harness your power without fear and transmute that energy into what best serves you. I set the intention that you remember your worthiness of recovery. You are worthy of loving and thriving.

KaSandra Turner

I hope you love you without apology. Take what is yours unapologetically. Reclaim your divinity through your own authentic self-expression.

We are Eden.

Made in the USA
Columbia, SC
20 May 2021